Sa rang hae!
(I Love You)

Ankita Verma

BookLeaf Publishing

India | USA | UK

Sa Rang Hae! (I Love You) © 2024 Ankita
Verma

All rights reserved.

No part of this publication may be
reproduced, stored in a retrieval system, or
transmitted, in any form or by any means,
electronic, mechanical, photocopying,
recording or otherwise, without the prior
written permission of the presenters.

Ankita Verma asserts the moral right to be
identified as the author of this work.

Presentation by *BookLeaf Publishing*

Web: www.bookleafpub.com

E-mail: info@bookleafpub.com

ISBN: 9789363310063

First edition 2024

*Dedicated to my love, my life, my husband,
Rohan!*

ACKNOWLEDGEMENTS

I would like to dedicate this book to the love of my life, my partner in crime, my husband Rohan, who is my pillar of strength! Thank you for believing in me and my dreams. It is only with your unconditional love and support that I could relive my dream of writing again! I would also like to thank my sisters Ajita and Aparajita, who are my lifelines. They have always guided me to do what feels right and have always inspired me to be a better person. Last but not least, I would like to thank my late mother, my guardian angel, from whom I got this creative gift. Mummy, you have always encouraged me to be the best version of myself, and I miss you so much every day!

PREFACE

Within the pages of this collection, you'll find a cocoon of emotions delicately woven into verse, capturing the essence of love in its myriad forms. From the tender embrace of first encounters to the bittersweet ache of longing, these poems illuminate the human experience of love in all its complexity and splendour. As you delve into these lines, may they resonate with the echoes of your own heart's whispers and kindle a flame that transcends the boundaries of time and space.

My Love

We were truly worlds apart,
I know it would have been very hard.
But when you came looking for me,
It was the Universe that couldn't let it be!

I remember the day we first met,
The sky looked so beautiful in a pink sunset.
A cool breeze swept across my face,
It seemed magical in time's embrace!

Then you smiled at me with your beautiful eyes,
And everything became so calm and nice.
You spoke and spoke all through the night,
With a cup of coffee in my hand
I listened and listened... Oh, what a sight!

Times passed by and we came closer,
Situations were tough, but we stuck together.
When reality hit me hard and I was in despair,
My sorrows too you were there to share.

Of all the hard times we've been through,
Never giving up to misery's woo!
I know it could have broken us apart,
But something kept us going on from the very
start.

Remembering the old times makes me smile,
Wish I could hold the moments just for a while!
For I miss the roses and you holding my hand,
I don't want 'us' to be a chapter written in sand!

I don't know what love is and probably never
will,
But when I close my eyes and stay still.
I think of you as a part of me,
Then I realise that this is love, and it was always
meant to be!

You are my hope, my biggest strength,
It will never change throughout my life's length.
As they say, love should be unconditional and
true,
I know if I can be, I can only be with you...

I love you!

Never Without You

Waking up every day with you by my side,
You look so serene; it fills me with pride.
To have a heart so pure to cherish and love,
My wish being granted from high above.

Brewing the morning coffee with you,
Your sweet smile is the best morning view.
With a warm hug and a sweet kiss,
Life seems complete with nothing amiss.

The everyday struggles seem so small,
With you, together we can conquer them all.
The small joys in life that we share,
Living in the moment without a care.

Even in the disagreements and fights,
I never want to let you out of my sight.
Letting bygones be bygones, we begin with a
fresh start,
For not even destiny can do us apart.

I cannot imagine my life without you,
You paint my life with beautiful hues.
I promise to love you forever and more,
Like the sand that flows but never leaves its
shore!

Eternity

In you, I see my life, sweetheart,
Not even destiny can do us apart,
My world revolves around your sweet smile,
That makes my heart beat for just another while.

Like the star that shines bright in the sky,
And the cool, fragrant breeze that passes by.
My life gets a meaning I don't know why,
From your love, dear, that will never die.

I have reasons to miss you night and day,
To see you in my dreams and say,
'You are my love, my life, my destiny,
And I'll stake everything for you, my honey'!

In the mountains of sighs,
In the oceans of cries,
I see you as my way,
To eternity that will never sway!

Faith

A gentle thread that intertwines two hearts,
With a promise of love, a new life starts.
On an unseen path, a journey begins,
Like an unsung song, the blessed soul sings.

Dreams are dreamt with a blindfold on,
Plans are made from dusk till dawn.
Without an assurance of what might be,
Surpassing every sorrow with a feeling of glee.

This undying feeling of hope and belief,
In each other's ability to surpass any grief.
To stand by each other come what may,
To an undying trust that can never sway.

This is what faith is all about,
That love will conquer all without a doubt.
In God's will, my faith remains strong,
That in each other's hearts is where we actually
belong!

Sometimes

Sometimes I wish you were here,
Sometimes I wish you were more near,
Sometimes I wish to love you more,
Sometimes I wish I could be all yours!

Sometimes I wish to see you in my eyes,
Sometimes I wish to feel you in my smile,
Sometimes I wish to touch you in an endless
span,
Sometimes I wish to do everything for you that I
can.

Sometimes I wish to name this life to you,
Sometimes I wish to name the others too.
Sometimes I wish to deserve your love and care,
But sometimes I think life is not so fair.

Sometimes I wish you could sense my feelings,
Sometimes I wish you could give my life a
meaning.

But sometimes I wish to give my illusions a
reality,
That you would never be mine in life's
atrocities.

Well! Am I not worth your attention?
Then why this ignorance, or are these your mere
pretensions?
My life starts and ends with you,
I need a fair trial
But as you say, 'Love is not enough for one's
survival'.

You and I

We are so similar yet poles apart,
There is an untold connection, heart to heart.
I like to stay hidden; you like to shine,
But our connection makes me trust in the
Divine.

You are brave and feisty while I am quiet and
shy,
I am like the ocean, and you are like the sky up
high.
It was impossible for our life paths to meet,
But destiny had already made her plans indeed.

I look in your eyes and I see a familiar soul,
That is no different from what I inside hold.
I feel we have known each other for lifetimes,
Like a poem that is written with perfect rhymes.

Even though we are different on the outside,
We share the same values and morals with pride.

I know you don't believe in destiny but I do,
There was no one else made for me but only
you!

If Only

Fingers intertwined, we walked hand in hand,
Not a care in the world, no future planned.
Clinging on to promises untold,
Not knowing how our lives would unfold!

Looking into each other's eyes, we smiled,
A bond of unbreakable trust we signed.
In which I was yours and you were always mine,
Like the stars that lit up the sky with their shine.

Passing through the crossroads of life,
Destiny brought us to a new strife.
From then on, we had different paths to tread,
Leaving behind the lives we once lead.

With a promise to find each other once again,
We let go of each other in agony and pain.
If only we knew there was a way to be,
Letting each other soar in the sky wild and free!

Part of Me

There is a feeling in my heart I can't describe,
Whenever I think of you, I can't help but smile.
If you understand what I am going through,
You can call it anything, but it should start with
you!

I have embraced a beautiful wish for so long,
I need not say it because you know where my
heart belongs!
Your name is written on every breath of mine,
Our connection is orchestrated by the Divine!

Our story was written in the stars,
Even destiny could not keep us apart.
We complement each other like night and day,
I'll prove my love for you in a million ways.

I will always think of you with that same sweet
smile,

Still chasing your dreams with those beautiful
eyes.
And the one truth that will always be,
Is that I'll always love you as you are now a part
of me!

Unconditional Love

When I told you last time that we should move
on,
There can be no more 'us', so let bygones be
bygones,
You too agreed as if that's what even you wanted
all along,
Strangely, unlike other times, I too didn't wish I
was wrong.

I smiled, I laughed, I spoke out of turn,
I did everything to run away from the real
heartburn.
I kept telling myself that I was mighty strong,
But my heart knew what it missed, why I was
wrong.

So I forced myself to think of all the things I
hated,
The times when I felt mistreated and
disrespected.
Of all the fights and arguments that made me
cry,
I felt so alone that even my tears went dry.

So I convinced myself that I did the right thing,
That I had enslaved myself like a bird without
wings.
I was full of pride, I felt elated,
I congratulated myself even though it was
belated.

But the very next moment something drew upon
me,
The anger evaporated, and I could clearly see.
That you did what you did for the reasons best
known to you,
I too had reasons for what I did, what I had to
do.

I could no longer feel the pain within me,
I was liberated, I could just let myself be.
That's when I realised I had a different view,
I wanted your true happiness; I wanted you to be
you!

With mistakes and regrets up my sleeve,
I've learnt to let go of my long-held beliefs.
Except for one that love makes you whole and
beautiful truly,
And I realised this now when I knew I loved you
unconditionally.

I hope one day you love yourself the way I love
you,
Walk past all your insecurities and inabilities to
find the real you.
To live this life fully and fall in love once again,
Do this, live happily, and I'll know my love
didn't go in vain!

One Glance!

The only thing I crave for,
Maybe it's the thing I'll even die for.
Nobody in this world knows it better than you,
Then why do you seem so ignorant and aloof.

Every time I see you passing by,
My heart gives yet another sigh!
But you always seem to be in an untold haste,
Not knowing, oh dear! My head is no more in
place.

Yesterday night I saw you and me hand in hand,
Walking past the soft breeze and the cold sand.
You lit the darkness with your bright smile,
Oh, how I wished we could walk for just another
mile!

You look so beautiful in that pink dress,
I am left with no words for you to impress,
But you know my heart speaks all the love for
you,
You may never understand it, but I know it's
true.

Every day I start with a brand new hope,
With which I am just able to cope,
All the pain and cries of your ignorance,
For I am just waiting for your… One Glance!

Worth

Living life is an art,
I knew this when I came closer to your heart.
But today I find myself miles away from you,
From that heart and that soul too!

I'll love you forever, you know this,
Your touch and warmth are all that I miss.
Yet you ignore this and seem to say,
Dear, feel me in your loneliness and dismay.

In your love, sweetheart, was this my destiny?
Was this true love or my insanity?
But I know that I love you eternally,
And I'll cherish each moment of my heartbreak
happily!

I secretly pray for this phase to end,
So that we could be together and make all the
amends.
You are a God's gift I'll always treasure,
Your worth in my life can't be measured.

Happy Love

Smile takes over, leaving no place for a frown,
Making faces together looking like clowns.
Giving each other a silent treatment after every
fight,
But coming back to each other, trying to make it
right!

Where every moment is filled with fun,
And nothing can pull us down under the sun.
Talking to each other for hours at length,
Repeated conversations, still they never end!

Thinking of one another even in the mundane
things,
We are bound to each other with an invisible
string.
Like two lost souls have found their way,
To each other's hearts like night and day!

In all the joy and merriness around,
We still hear each other's silent pain's sound.

With a little prayer to the Almighty, a promise
we send,
To take away any teardrop of my sweetheart, my
best friend!

Mine

I feel like I've known you all along,
Your eyes, your smile, your smell seem like a
familiar song.
When I look at you, I can't help but smile,
The kind of smile that I haven't smiled in a
while.

With you, I want to rediscover myself once
again,
To go to a place in my heart where there was
once pain.
And rip open that part and let you in,
To let go of the past and allow a new journey to
begin.

To take your hand in mine and let you know,
You feel like a sweet warmth on a day full of
snow.

To hold you so close that our heartbeats become
one,
To make you feel at home as if no more battles
need to be won.

As I stand here, I make this promise to you,
I can't show you how much, but I know I'll
always love only you.
So with a kiss, I seek your permission to be
mine,
For you are my star; for me, you'll always shine!

Soulmates

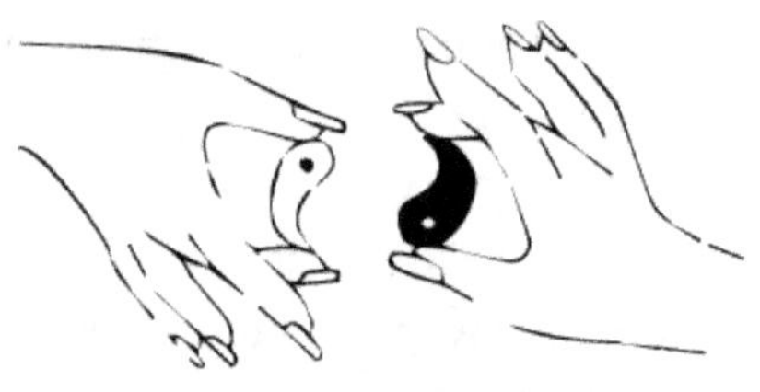

Through moments of truth and time's embrace,
Two souls begin their journey in Divine Grace.
Destiny weaves its intricate design,
Guided to one another, their paths align.

In the ebbs and flows of life's sweet dance,
Soulmates search for their soul's true romance.
Across the miles and through oceans wide,
Their hearts beat as one, always side by side.

Chasing the odds through a divine encounter,
Their souls meet, and hearts begin to ponder.
In a fleeting gaze and a slight glance,
Two souls become one; time stands still in a
trance.

They walk together through life's road,
In joy and sorrow, they share each other's load.
In laughter and tears, they find their way,
That with a smile on their face, they can conquer
each day.

In each other's heart, they find their home,
They may be apart but never alone.
For their bond is engraved in love's eternal
flame,
A written testimony to destiny's sweet claim.

Soulmates are companions, confidants, lovers
and more,
In each other's arms, they fight the uproars.
Of sadness, loss, heartbreaks and despair,
Assuring each other that life's never fair!

Cherry Blossom

Sitting on a bench in spring's embrace,
Everything looks so surreal by nature's grace.
Soft breeze blows across your face in a gentle
trance,
Which makes the blossoms flutter in a delightful
dance.

What a sight it is to behold,
Every petal has a story that needs to be told.
Floating away under the beautiful bright sky,
Lovers of beauty, stay still and softly sigh!

In that moment of ephemeral glow,
Hearts become full with nowhere to go.
With a feeling of belongingness that is sweet and
rare,
Living life in its glory without a care!

A sad feeling dawns on me, wishing you were
here,
To catch the passing breeze so cosy and dear.
The only desire in my heart remains,
Is to watch the cherry blossoms with you in
timeless reign!

Quiet Romance

In the everyday rush of life,
Where everyone is stuck in their own strife.
Everybody is searching for a second chance,
But the answer lies in a quiet romance!

No words are spoken; only souls converse,
With a calm demeanour, silent moments
immerse.
Soft whispers sweep across timelines,
There is no place for pretence; only innocence
shines.

Promises aren't made; they are fulfilled,
Dreams aren't chased; they are together built.
Where love is expressed not only in words
refined,
But through acts and deeds that are not
pre-designed.

With every touch, we take a silent vow,
To live in the present in the here and now.
In starlight's gleam, our love does the dance,
For in each other, we have found our quiet
romance!

Love and forgiveness

In the garden of forgiveness, love blooms bright,
Where tender petals of understanding take flight.
Through storms of hurt and pain, we find our
way,
Guided by compassion with each passing day.

Forgiveness mends the bridge once torn and
tender,
Mending wounds through grace and surrender.
In its embrace, hearts find their solace and
peace,
Rendering compassion to erase all its crease.

Let kindness be the melody, forgiveness the
song,
In love's symphony, where we all belong.
For in forgiving, we set ourselves free,
To love again, as boundless as the sea.

So let us dance in the rhythm of grace,
Embracing forgiveness in every embrace.
For love knows no bounds, no limit and no end,
In its vast expanse, forgiveness is our friend!

Letting Go

In the saga of true love, sometimes we find,
There is a need to let go, leaving the past behind.
In deep agony and with immense heartache,
One learns to let go, not knowing what the
future awaits.

For clinging on to the past will bring only pain,
So release it and feel free, like dancing in the
rain.
With a heavy heart and tears that no one can see,
Not knowing what was and will be.

Remember, letting go is not a sign of defeat,
It is ruthless, courageous, bold and sweet.
Trust the process and reset your heart,
For love to find you again, never again to part.

So open your soul to let the love flow in,
Embracing the beauty of letting go, dive within.
When you accept yourself, new love may bloom,
That is promised for a lifetime, with nothing to
assume!

Sunset on the Beach

As the sun bids the day farewell,
Upon the beach, a tale to tell.
Golden hues kiss the tranquil sea,
A symphony of serenity!

The waves caress the sandy shore,
Whispering secrets forevermore.
Seagulls dance in the fading light,
In a spectacle of pure delight.

With each passing moment, colours blend,
In nature's masterpiece, without end.
Oranges, pinks and purples ignite the sky,
As the day gracefully says goodbye.

Footprints in the sand, a silent trace,
Of memories made in this sacred space.
As the sun dips below the horizon's reach,
We cherish the beauty of the sunset on the
beach.

Wishing Star

Staring at the infinite mighty canvas,
Where millions of stars shine in their grandness,
With a passing gaze, there is a beam of light,
Leading us to the wishing star, distant and
bright.

A ray of hope arises in every heart,
That chances upon the wishing star.
Where unfulfilled dreams are sent across the
horizon so high,
And rests at the point where wishes touch the
sky.

For in its ephemeral glow,
It makes the mortal desires flow.

Distant hearts that forever yearn,
Pray to the wishing star for their faith to return.

As I stand still in its beauty and grace,
It feels like being teleported with you to another
space.
Where our dreams turn to hope and hope to
reality,
Where we promise to love each other till
immortality!

Innocent Love

He was only nine,
When the first love letter he signed,
To the girl who lived next door,
Because she was young, pretty and bright

He had expected a good, long reply,
But he was destined to sigh,
As the letter he could not part,
To his one and only sweetheart!

He tore the letter and wrote again and again,
But all his efforts went off in vain,
Sometimes his love was not expressed,
And sometimes his grammar made him
depressed.

He thought to take help from his father,
Who showed less brilliance and much youth
rather?
But he said he was busy with his life
Writing love letters to his divorced wife.

But the boy did not lose heart,
He was determined to do his part.
So he decided to take inspiration from Romeo
and Juliet,
But sat reading it like an idiot!

Frustrated, he decided to hear a romantic song,
But sorry to say he was mercilessly wrong.
The song was of the Latin age,
Which made him cry out his lungs in rage!

He then thought of his friend in need,
Who was very experienced in these matters
indeed!
He searched for him day and night,
Alas! Found him with his girl, charming and
bright!

Forbidden Love

In your eyes, my world shines so bright,
With you, I soar, I shine and everything seems
right.
My true self emerges, free and bold,
There is no need to hide that my heart beats
manifold.

With you, I find my inner voice,
My shy soul finally speaks and makes some
noise.
You help me find my own worth,
By embracing myself truly, with joy and mirth.

But alas, I know our love is not meant to be,
Worldly bounds restrict you and me.
I dare not speak my heart's desire,
Lest the world, our love, would tire.

Your smile, a radiant work of art,
Lights up my world and captures my heart.
Your carefree soul, a joy to see,
Where a responsible heart beats secretly.

I know you battle demons, dark and deep,
I cannot fight them for you, so I silently weep.
I promise to be by your side through every strife,
Loving you, in secret and for life.

Our love, pure and true, yet concealed,
A hidden flame that dare not reveal.
But know this, my love, I'll always be,
Yours, in heart, in soul, in secrecy.

Our Home

A home, where dreams and hopes are made,
Where years of love, hope and laughter are
shared.
You and I, hand in hand, side by side,
In our haven, where love and togetherness
reside.

We cling to each other through joy and strife,
Our bond, unbreakable; a lifelong rife.
Living in our home, a sanctuary we've always
adored,
A cosy nest, where our love forever soars.

We savour coffee's warmth in our quiet nook,
Grateful for the blessings, living life like an
open book.
Our courtyard blooms, with children's playful
cheers,
Sunbeams dance through windows and wipe
away our tears.

In this sweet haven, we create our own world,
And guard it with barriers, letting no worries be
heard.
Our refuge, our peace, where weary days
subside,
In each other's arms, we gently reside.

Free minds, rested souls, in harmony entwined,
Let's build this home, where our love forever
shines.
Together we'll grow in joy and age,
In our dream home, where love turns every
page.

Counting On You

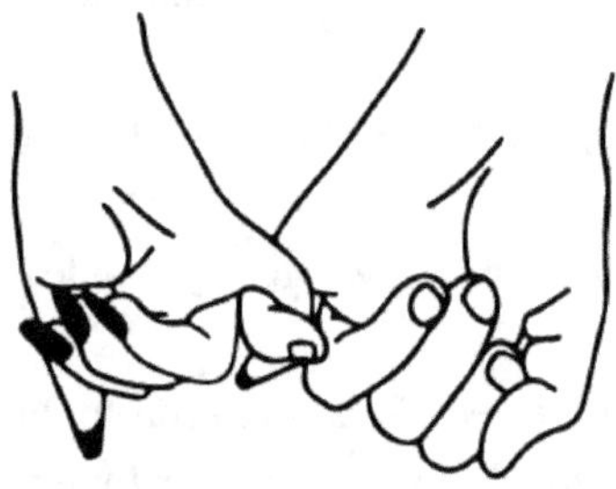

In life's uncertain tapestry, you're my steadfast
thread,
A reassuring presence, where love and trust are
wed.
Through trials and tribulations, you stand by my
side,
A rock of strength, where fears and doubts
subside.

When darkness descends and stars hide from
view,
Your guiding light shines bright, like a freshly
dropped dew.
In turbulent seas, you are the calm and peaceful
shore,
A refuge where my weary heart finds rest once
more.

With every breath, I count on you to be,
A constant companion, through life's ecstasy.

Through laughter and tears, through joys and
fears,
You're the safe haven, the song my heart hears.

Your unwavering support, a beacon in the night,
Illuminates my path, banishing life's plight.
With you, my heart beats stronger, free and true,
Together, forever, our love shines through.

In your loving arms, I find my solace and peace,
A sense of belonging, my soul is finally
released.
Counting on you through life's joys and sorrows,
I will love you unconditionally, like there is no
tomorrow.

A Heartfelt Confession

In silence, I've hidden my pain,
Afraid to share, I have locked it in vain.
But don't blame yourself, dear love; the pain is
mine,
A weight I've carried since childhood's troubled
shrine.

Unspoken tears and unhealed scars,
Festered within behind guarded bars.
With your arrival like the sunshine so bright,
You healed my heart, banishing my endless
night.

Yet sometimes old fears resurface, and I retreat,
But with you near, my heart finds courage in
every heartbeat.
Having you by my side, I get up and face my
demons again,
Your love is my shield, my strength; I have
nothing to lose in the bargain.

With you, each day is worth the fight,
Even gloomy skies shine with your loving light.
You know my secrets but you choose to love me
still,
Treating me like royalty with your generous
will.

My heart wanders for you like an eagle soaring
high,
But in your arms, I have found my peaceful sky.
I owe you this lifetime and all that's to come,
Our love story is written up in the stars that
cannot be undone.

I have always loved you like a burning flame,
Too deep for words, it echoes through my name.
With every breath, I'll prove that my love for
you is true,
Forever and ever, my heart will always belong to
you.

Our Little Miracle

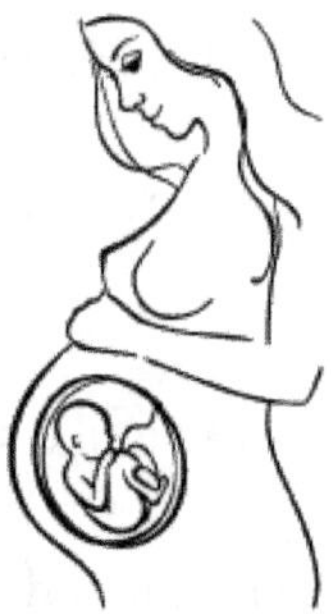

In joy, we welcome our firstborn's smile,
A feeling so precious, worth a lifetime's while.
Our hearts entwined in love's purest form,
A gift from above, a treasure to transform.

It is God's greatest creation, a life so divine,
A symbol of our love, forever intertwined.
With every glance, our souls take flight,
In this little one, our love shines bright.

No words can express the joy we share,
Luckiest souls, with love beyond compare.
This tiny hand holds our destiny,
A legacy born of love and harmony.

With each passing day, our hearts swell,
Pride and wonder our love will tell.
We'll nurture, guide and set him free,
To conquer dreams wild and carefree.

Though someday he'll spread his wings,
And build a life where love and laughter sing.
We'll beam with pride through tears of delight,
Knowing we crafted a heart so caring and bright.

Our little one, our precious gem, our world.
Forever grateful for our prayers being heard.
In his eyes, our legacy will shine,
A reflection of our love so divine.

This bond we share an eternal tie,
A dance of love 'til the day we say goodbye.
But even then, a part of our hearts shall remain,
Entwined in his heart, filled with our love
forever sustained.

To Love and Beyond

In the fleeting glance of an eye,
Our souls collided, and eternity replied.
In that instant, I knew that I had finally found,
My soulmate, my love, filling my heart with joy
abound.

Through lifetimes, our love has nurtured and
grown,
Into an unbroken melody with an endless tone.
Though veils of time tried to be what was meant
to be,
But my soul recognised you beyond what our
eyes could see.

Sometimes our words can be a reflection of our
pain,
Which may pierce the heart, but the love
remains.
For in the depths of our troubled sea,
One can see the shores of love meant for just
you and me.

A defence mechanism, a shield to hide,
Your vulnerability, your heart inside.
But I see beyond the armour and the pride,
To the love we share, where our hearts finally
reside.

Our bond transcends the tests of time,
Unconditional, pure and sublime.
No force, no fear, no doubt can part,
Our souls intertwined forever in each other's
heart.

Through every storm every darkest night,
My love for you will shine like a guiding light.
In your eyes, my soul finds its solace and peace,
In your arms, all my pain and sorrow cease.

This love defies the bounds of space,
An infinite dance, a sacred, secret place.
To love and beyond, I'll follow you,
Through every lifetime, my heart belongs to
you.

When You Know, You Know

In uncharted waters, our eyes first met,
Strangers bound by an unseen debt.
The air was thick with unfamiliarity,
Yet, a spark of recognition sets our hearts free.

A strange, unspoken energy pulsed between,
A sense of déjà vu, as if we had always been.
Connected to each other in some past life,
Our souls are like two lost pieces finding their tribe.

With each touch, a long-lost flame ignited,
And as we spoke, our hearts were more than delighted.
With rhythms of similarity, echoes of our past,
In each other's eyes, we saw our true selves forecast.

Flaws and imperfections, yet we couldn't ignore,
That our hearts whispered, 'This is what we're
looking for'.
A love not based on logic or reason's sway,
But an instinctual knowing of belongingness
come what may.

Secret smiles, stolen glances and gentle gazes,
Conveyed truths about our love story in phases.
Your eyes, a window to your loving soul,
Reflected the depth of emotions felt but yet
untold.

In realms beyond, our love is like a star that
shines
Entrusted in a bond that transcends the mundane
confine.
No ulterior motives, no hidden agendas thrive
Just pure love keeping our hearts alive.

The shy smile, the unsaid words, the
unexpressed pain,
Create a suspense that's both lovely and insane.
Addictive longing, a bittersweet refrain,
Echoes through my being like a sweet strain.

In the magic rush, and madness of it all,
I'm lost, yet found, in the depths of your loving
call.
My heart, a fragile, quivering thing,
Beats solely for you, my love, my everything.

When you know, you know, and I know it's true,
In all the depths of life, my heart belongs to you.
No logic, no reason, just an instinctual sigh,
In your love, my heart finds its eternal sky.

A Heart's Uncharted Territory

When souls collide, a cosmic dance begins,
A strange familiarity, where magic spins.
Two strangers, bound by unseen ties,
A heart's connection, a sweet surprise.

One walks aimlessly into the depths of the night
Yet in this darkness a kindred spirit light.
Two souls meet like a beautiful tapestry
intricately woven,
With a love so sacred, deep and unspoken.

A secret glance, a knowing smile,
Eyes that speak volumes for miles and miles.
A connection symbolising a love so true,
A heart that yearns and yearns only for you.

Fragile heart, it sees no logic's might,
It just knows the one; it's the guiding light.
In realms unseen, it searches for a soul so dear,
A love so pure, dispelling all the fears.

No hidden agendas, no selfish gain,
A love so selfless, a heart so sane.
Shy smiles, unspoken words, blessed with
Divine's grace,
A suspenseful longing, hoping for a sweet
embrace.

The magic, the rush, the insanity,
Missing someone without a reason why.
An addictive pull to fulfil a heart's desire,
Lost in the depths of emotions, hearts that never
lose their fire.

Rainbow

Love is like a rainbow, vibrant and bright,
Seven colours shining, a wondrous sight.
Joy, happiness, trust, faith, loyalty, respect and
intimacy
Are the different hues that define its vibrancy.

In your eyes, the colours blend and merge,
A kaleidoscope of emotions emerges.
You are the rainbow that has brightened my sky,
A treasure trove of love, passing me by.

You are the sunshine after the rain,
A radiant beam that chases away all of my pain.
Your presence illuminates my world with a
radiant glow
Leading my heart to a world I have never seen
but already know.

In your presence, these colours of love unfold,
Like a beautiful painting filled with emotions
untold.

In your touch, joy overflows within me like a
stream,
My happiness knows no bounds; with you, I live
my wildest dream.

Trust's gentle whisper, faith's steadfast stand,
Loyalty's unwavering loving hand.
Respect's soft gaze, intimacy's warm embrace,
In your love, I find my sacred space.

If only you knew the depth of my heart,
The love I hold for you, then we'd never be
apart.
You are the rainbow that shines so bright,
My world is filled with vibrant colours in your
loving light.

Be mine, dear rainbow; let our love grow and
shine,
Together we'll dance beneath the stars and age
like fine wine.
So listen to me when I say
Merge me with you and let it be the only way.

I miss you!

In your absence, I ache each day,
You are my world, my sunshine's ray.
My angel, my rock, my everything true,
Life without you is unimaginable, sad and blue.

Love's journey can be rough and long,
But with you, my heart beats strong.
Your presence makes everything alright,
A gentle calm that soothes my night.

The thought of you brings joyful tears,
Of moments we'll share through all our years.
No need for words, no need for deeds,
Just sitting with you quietly, I am almost freed.

Hours melt away lost in your eyes,
In your arms, my soul finds its surprise.
A haven where I am free to be,
With you, my love is where I'm meant to be.

My love for you is beyond words and it only
grows,
Infinite and pure as the morning glows.
If fate allowed, I'd name each lifetime of mine,
Yours eternally, my soulmate divine.

You are my universe, vast and wide,
My galaxies, where stars reside.
My one and only, my guiding light,
Forever and always, my love shines bright.

In your love, I find my peaceful nest,
With you, my heart finds its eternal rest.
Together, our love will forever thrive,
A love so strong, it touches the sky.

Secretive Heart

In hidden truths, my soul takes flight,
Concealing my love in this silent night.
Afraid to speak the truth, I veil my heart,
Lest rejection tears our love story apart.

In shadows that cast above, I quietly adore,
Guarding my feelings from everyone evermore.
But with every beat, my heart confesses,
To be yours forever in secret addresses.

Your eyes like a mystic mirror show,
The image of our destiny that few may know.
In the depths of our love, I light a sacred flame,
That burns bright, yet hidden from life's game.

When questioned about you, I deny the spark,
Protecting our love, leaving everyone in the
dark.

But when I look at you, my face shows with a subtle hidden sign,
Revealing the truth of my heart, something I cannot feign.

Living with these beautiful lies in a velvet disguise,
Concealing the love that fills my secret eyes.
So, till eternity, I'll silently wait,
For the day you will uncover our love's hidden fate.

Unseen Love

Before our eyes met, my heart knew you,
A smile within, a flutter grew.
In butterflies' gentle dance, I would see,
Your presence near, though miles apart, you
would be.

When I saw you, Destiny whispered, 'You're
meant to be',
My soul recognised your soul and said, 'This
love will set you free'.
Among countless souls, I searched in vain,
But none compared to you, a longing of sweet
pain.

My heart beats for you I know this much is true,
In every beauty, I felt my love, and it only grew.
In flowers' sweet scent, I sensed your grace,
In the rainbows' vibrant hues, I felt your gentle
face.

Angels carried messages from above,
Reminding me of our eternal love.
In every sunrise, I felt your glow,
In stars that twinkle, I felt our love grow.

My heart feels light, my soul takes flight,
Imagining you as my guiding light.
You're my best friend, soulmate and confidant,
true,
My lover, my everything – my heart belongs to
you.

When fate brings us face to face,
I know I'll recognise you without any haste
No obstacles will then keep us apart,
Together forever, it will be our love's shining
start.

Till then I'll find you in life's delight,
In beauty's splendour and your loving light.
In every breeze, your whispers I'll hear,
My unseen love, forever drawing near.

Can't wait to see you

As morning breaks, my eyes, once heavy with
sleep,
Now sparkle bright, and my heart begins to leap.
The thought of meeting you, my love so true,
Awakens me with a vigour, and my soul renews.

I rise with joy and a smile on my face,
And choose the dress that's been saved for this
special place.
The music sways with a gentle, loving breeze,
As I prepare to leave, my heart dances in sweet
ease.

No hunger pangs, just butterflies inside,
Anticipation builds; my love, I cannot hide.
I drive through meadows green and concrete
grey,
My heart aflame; love shines through every step
of the way.

The playlist whispers secret songs that speak
your name,
Reminding me of you and our love's sweet
sacred flame.
I envision scenes of us together holding hands,
Gazing into each other's eyes, walking in the
sand.

Promises of eternity with vows to never part,
In every travesty, our love will find a brand-new
start.
In special times and in mundane, our love
remains,
Eternal and constant through life's joys and
pains.

As I journey to you, thoughts race with glee,
Of our reunion, that's meant to be.
The biggest warmest embrace in this world so
wide,
From you, my love, there is nothing more to
hide.

I love you more with each passing day,
Through every breath, in every way.
In your love, my soul finds its home,
Forever with you, my heart will roam.

The Missing Piece

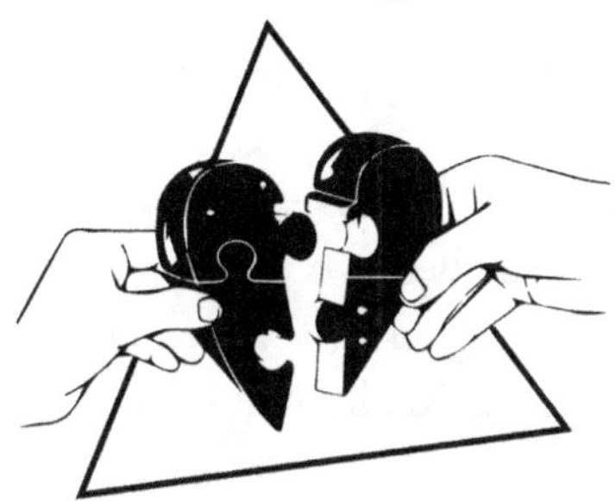

You entered our lives, like a shining light,
A saviour we never knew, a precious sight.
Filling our voids, healing wounds of the past,
Bringing stability in our lives, peace that will
forever last.

Years of struggle, tears and lonely nights,
Vanished in an instant with your warm delights.
A rock, a support you mean so much more,
Now our family's whole; you are someone we
truly adore.

My father's pride, his warrior true,
He beams with joy, with love shining through.
My sisters cherish you with hearts so pure,
Sometimes I think they love you more!

But amidst this world of joy, a tear I shed,
For my mother, who didn't get to meet you
instead.

She would have loved you dearly with all her
heart,
And cherished you from the very start.

But I'll give you that love, that care, that light,
The warmth you deserve, through day and night.
You're a special soul, a wonderful man,
A treasure that is so rare in this world's plan.

You guide us through life's ups and downs,
With your love, our hearts wear no frowns.
No challenge too great, no test too bold,
All battles are won as our bright future unfolds.

I love you more with each passing day,
For being the one who showed us the way.
You're the missing piece that made us whole,
Forever in our hearts, our love for you will
unfold.

We Stand as One

Even at our lowest, faced with despair's dark
night,
We found hope flickering still, a beacon shining
bright.
We are bound to each other with an unbroken
bond,
Together we rise; our spirits fly to eternity and
beyond.

There is no going back or surrendering to the
pain,
For we are each other's world, and our love
sustains.
In an unfair and unkind world, we find our
strength
By being at each other's side, we live our life's
length.

I've seen us struggle and felt helpless too,
But faith in us and God sees us through.

For when we're together, nothing can stand
Against the power of our love, we fight hand in
hand.

Times may be hard with challenges untold,
But a higher power guides us young and old.
As we grow, we'll look back and clearly see,
How protected and blessed we've always been.

Invincible in love, our hearts we have won all
the battles,
Dancing in the moonlight like stars, we dazzle.
I cherish our unconditional love with tender
care,
And hold a promise that all happiness and
sorrows will be shared.

Through lifetimes, I'll love you and stand by
your side,
Together we'll weather life's ebb and tide.
For with you, my love, I know we'll always be,
One in hope, one in faith, for eternities to see.

Reflection of You

Wherever I wander, wherever I roam,
Your presence surrounds me like a gentle home.
In daylight's warmth and darkest skies,
I see your face like a loving surprise.

In joyous moments, I behold your grin,
In despair's depths, your comfort draws near
within.
In thrilling experiences and mundane tasks,
Your image lingers forever clear and
unmasked...

With morning's coffee, rich and bold,
I taste your love, a flavour to unfold.
Each morsel I savour, each bite I take,
Reminds me of you, for our love's sake.

In empty streets, where solitude reigns,
Your sweet presence soothes my heart's pains.

In bustling markets vibrant and alive,
I glimpse your smile, and my soul thrives.

Every conversation is like a whispered tone,
Echoes your voice with a love forever known.
In happiness and joy, I see your face,
A radiant beam illuminating the empty space.

Laughter's bursts, tears' gentle flow,
All reflect your love as it ebbs and grows.
Each breath I take, each sigh I make,
Is a testament to our love's unbreakable sake.

In every gaze, our eyes entwine,
A love so strong, it transcends time and space's
design.
I've lost myself yet found my way,
To become a reflection of you, day by day.

Our bond is inseparable, a union true,
We're now one soul, in all we do.
I'm no longer myself, but you in me,
A mirrored love, for all eternity.

This is our love's profound declaration,
A bond that weaves our hearts in every creation.
I see you everywhere, in all I do,
For in your love, my heart beats anew.

If Everything Falls Apart

In shattered moments, when worlds collide,
And chaos reigns, with hearts full of pride,
I'll stand by you through every test of time,
Together we'll face the darkest of rhymes.

No chasm deep, no mountain high and wide,
Can come between us; my love will be your
guide.
Through life's turmoil, I'll be your peaceful
shore,
Your pillar of strength, forever and more.

Life's journey's not easy, with twists and turns,
But with me by your side, your heart will learn,
To face each dawn, with hope in every ray,
For I believe in you, come what may.

When the world crashes down and fears arise,
I'll be the one who'll lift your weary eyes,
To see the beauty in our love's pure light,
A bond so strong, forged in the darkest night.

In every moment, I'll pray for you,
And seek the blessings of a love so true,
I'll travel unknown roads through joy and strife,
To keep you safe and be your partner in life.

Our love's divine, a gift from above,
A treasure entrusted, in the beauty of our love,
In a world of uncertainty, we've found a shore,
Where love resides that forever we'll adore.

Imagine a life where our paths didn't cross,
But fate intervened, and our hearts were lost,
In the tapestry of time, our love's a work of art,
A masterpiece, crafted by a loving heart.

Now that we've met, our love will forever shine,
A beacon in darkness, an emotion so sublime,
In your eyes, my heart finds a home,
With you, I am never alone.

So when shadows fall and fears draw near,
Remember, my love, my presence is always
clear,
I'll hold your hand through life's ebb and flow,

Together, our love will conquer and forever
grow.

75

Whenever you are near

In your presence, I find my peaceful nest,
A sense of fulfilment and security; I am blessed.
With you by my side, my heart feels complete,
Reflecting on what truly matters, my soul
retreats.

Trivial things that once consumed my time and
space,
Fade away as your love takes its rightful place.
Pain and sorrow disappear from sight,
As your face lights up my world, shining so
bright.

Your presence makes my heart gleam with
delight,
Unbridled pleasure and happiness, a love so true
and bright.

With you, everything falls into place,
My love for you, a flame that time and space
won't erase.

Even in distance, my love for you remains,
A constant reminder of the heart's deep pains.
But whenever you're near, my love shines bold,
A physical manifestation, my heart's treasure to
hold.

With you, I face my demons, unafraid and
strong,
Together we conquer, right where we belong.
I love you till eternity and beyond,
A love so profound, it transcends all bounds.

Your love is my happiness, my joy and guiding
light,
Gratitude fills my heart for our love's pure sight.
Thankful to God for bringing us together,
Forever entwined, our love will weather.

I love you more with each passing day,
An endless ocean, my love for you will sway.
Through life's ups and downs, I'll cherish and
adore,
Forever and always, my love, my heart belongs
to you.

Calling onto you

When fears and doubts assail my soul,
And loneliness seems to take its toll,
I pause, take a breath and whisper low,
Your name, my refuge, my heart's sweet home.

In the stillness, I feel your gentle hand,
A reassuring presence, across the land,
My anxieties, like autumn leaves, fade fast,
As thoughts of you envelop me forever to last.

Your face, a radiant beacon, shines so bright,
Illuminating life's darkest, most troubled night,
With you, my love, all things seem possible and
true,
My heart, once heavy, now soars anew.

Time stands still as I behold your loving gaze,
My world, once chaotic, now finds a peaceful
daze,
In your arms, I find solace, my haven and nest,
Forever with you, my love, is where I rest.

You are my destiny, my guiding star,
My everything, near or far,
Life without you is unimaginable and grey,
A canvas without colour, a song without a sway.

I cherish you not for what you do,
But for who you are, my love, pure and true,
No earthly delight or trial can take me away,
From the love we share, our bond, come what
may.

In joy and sorrow, I call upon your name,
My saviour, beloved, angel in disguise, my
claim,
You soothe my pain, calm every troubled sea,
Forever my shelter, my love, my destiny.

Through life's ebb and flow, I'll hold on tight,
To the love we share, our beacon in the night,
Together we'll brave life's joys and fears,
Forever entwined, our love, through laughter
and tears.

Eternal Completeness

In your presence, I am made whole,
With a sense of unity, I reach my heart's deepest
goal.
With you near, my soul feels complete,
No longing remains my love, my sweet retreat.

You are my world, my guiding light,
My heart swells with pride, day and night.
Thoughts of you envelop me like a warm and
gentle breeze,
Your nearness is like a comforting solace, my
heart's ease.

The moon's soft glow, a beacon in the night,
Reminds me of your presence, a love so bright.
In its serene light, I feel your gentle hand,
A reassuring touch across this vast land.

You are God's blessing, a gift, so pure and true,
You, my love, the best, my heart's deepest cue.

No worldly treasure, no earthly delight,
Can compare to the love we share, our bond so
bright.

I'd move mountains and brave life's raging sea,
To keep you safe, to love and cherish thee.
Through every storm, I'll stand by your side,
Your confidant, support, through life's ebb and
tide.

Your happiness is my heart's sole desire,
A wish to see you thrive in our love's sweet
burning fire.
You deserve the world and all its delight,
My love, my everything, shining with all your
light.

In your eyes, my heart finds a home,
A refuge from life's turmoil, symbolising a love
forever grown.
Entwined as one our hearts in a single beat,
Play a symphony that is longingly sweet.

You are my forever, my love, my guiding star,
My soul's completion even from afar.
In your love, I find my peaceful rest,
Forever with you, my heart's eternal nest.

Beyond Illusions

In the realm of the heart, a paradox resides,
A love so unreal yet profoundly true, it abides.
Transcending imagination's bounds, it reigns,
A depth of emotion, fathomless, like an endless
plain.

Indescribable, this love, a symphony of the soul,
No words can capture its essence, its beauty
whole.
So I seek your eyes, a window to your heart,
To connect with your spirit and never depart.

In your gaze, I find solace, a haven of peace,
A gateway to your love, where my heart finds
release.
I yearn for you to seek my soul, to know me
true,
For in your love, I've found myself with nothing
due.

You already reside within my heart and soul,
No need to doubt, for it is the ultimate goal.
Someday, beyond illusions, you'll see,
The real me, and know the love I hold for thee.

This world may conjure illusions so our love
must disguise,
Away from the prying eyes like a constant
surprise.
Through life's distractions, I've walked past the
veil,
And found the truth of our love, an eternal,
endless tale.

For ages, I've loved you, unconditionally and
true,
Forever till eternity, you know my heart belongs
to you.
My life, my everything, I owe to your love's
might,
A debt of gratitude paid in full, through
eternity's sight.

No reassurance compares to the love I feel,
A conviction that guides me like an unwavering
zeal.
In your love, I find my haven, my peaceful nest,
With you, my heart beats as one in love's sweet
zest.

I love you, beyond words, beyond mortal sight,
In the realm of the soul, our love shines to our
soul's delight.

Smile and Tear

In the depths of the soul, where emotions roam,
Two companions dwell, a heartfelt home.
A smile and a tear together, they stay,
Reflecting the beauty of life's disarray.

With every laugh, a tear is born,
As joy and sorrow in harmony are sworn.
The smile, a radiant beam of delight,
Illuminates the path through the darkest night.

The tear, a glistening drop of the heart,
Falls softly like a work of art.
For in its clarity, our emotions shine,
A reflection of love forever divine.

Together they dance a waltz of the soul,
A symphony of feelings making us whole.
In moments of bliss or deepest pain,
Smiles and tears forever remain.

For what is joy without a hint of sorrow?
What is laughter without a tear to follow?
The smile and tear, a duet of the heart,
Expressing love never to depart.

Oh! smile and tear, my eternal friends,
Together forever till life's journey ends.
For in your bond, our emotions unfold,
Like a sky so vast with stories untold.

So let the smile and tear forever shine,
Like a beacon of love singing a heart's rhyme.
For in their harmony, we find our way,
To live through life's joys and sorrows, day by
day.

Bangles

In secret, I adorn my wrists with care,
Bangles that speak of love beyond compare.
A gift from you, my heart's sweet delight,
A token of our love that shines so bright.

I wear them every day with a hidden smile,
A coy glance, my heart dances for a while.
No one knows the story behind their shine,
But I feel your love, forever mine.

Restless days and sleepless nights I bear,
Longing to see your face, to feel you near.
My heart beats fast and my soul takes flight,
In dreams, our love shines like a guiding light.

With every chime of these bangles so fine,
Memories of you, my love, forever entwine.
In their melody, I hear your gentle voice,
Whispers of forever, a heartfelt choice.

Though I conceal the truth from prying eyes,
My heart reveals it in loving sighs.
These bangles remind me of our sweet embrace,
A love so strong that can never be erased.

So I'll wear them like a priceless treasure
A symbol of our love that cannot be measured.
And when we meet again, they will still adorn
My wrists with the same rhythm that cannot be
forgone.

Ring of promise

A circle of gold, a symbol so true,
A ring of promise given to you,
A token of love that will forever shine,
A bond between us, a blessing from the divine.

Every day a new memory is made,
As we colour our love story in every shade,
In joy and strife, through laughter and tears,
This ring reminds us that our love can conquer
all fears.

In its gentle curve, a promise is sealed,
A vow through which unconditional love is
revealed.
Through the depths of our love and the breadth
of our soul,
Our hearts are tied together and made whole.

The diamond signifies a light that burns bright,
A beacon of devotion, through day and night,
A guiding light that shines on our way,
Illuminating the path through life's busy day.

This ring of promise, a gift from my heart,
A symbol of forever that we'll never be apart,
Through time and space and every dimension,
Our love will always find its mention.

So, wear this ring close and hold it tight,
For it is a constant reminder of our love's might.
In its gentle warmth, may your heart find its
way,
To my heart, it's a constant companion that will
never sway.

Angel in disguise

In realms of fate, where stars align,
You appeared as my guardian divine,
A love so pure, a heart so true,
My angel, my love, forever shining through.

With wings of kindness, you enveloped me,
A shield of protection, a love that's free,
In your arms, I found my solace and peace,
A haven where my desires found their release.

Through life's turmoil, you stand by my side,
A constant presence, my guiding light,
On darkest nights, your love shines bright,
Illuminating the paths that banish my fright.

Your love, a flame that burns like a fire,
Warming my soul and lighting my heart's desire,
Unwavering loyalty that transcends the
judgements
Of prying eyes and unsheltered casements.

You are my rock, my shelter, my home,
Where I find refuge, and I am never alone,
Your love is a sanctuary, my safe haven
I feel so victorious, as if I never gave in.

So, with every breath, I'll love you till the end,
Through joys and sorrows, our hearts will
transcend,
Together we'll brave life's ebb and flow,
Hand in hand, our love will forever grow.

You, my guardian angel, my love so dear,
A treasure so precious, beyond compare,
In your eyes, my heart finds a home,
With you, my love, I am never alone.

So let us cherish this love we share,
A bond of trust, a promise beyond compare,
Forever connected in our hearts as one,
Together, we will conquer any travesties to
come.

You are my everything, my guiding light,
My shelter, my haven, my love, my sight,
In your love, I find my peaceful nest,
With you, my angel, I am forever blessed.

Guiding Star

In darkness when surrender beckons near,
And weary limbs refuse to persevere,
Inspiration's flame flickers, losing its might,
I gaze into your eyes and find my light.

Your unwavering faith, a beacon so bright,
Rekindles my soul, banishes the night,
Our love, an anchor, holds me fast,
A bond so strong, it forever lasts.

I rise for you, my guiding star,
Your love is my resilience near and far,
In your embrace I find the strength to face,
Life's cruelty its unfair and relentless pace.

Though victories may seem small and few,
With you, each triumph means the world anew,
You are my rock, my shelter from life's storm,
Together we brave the tempest's form.

Life's mysteries unfold beyond our sight,
But with you, my love, I'll hold on tight,
Through trials and tribulations, we'll stride,
Hand in hand, side by side.

Our love, pure, beautiful and true,
Endures through time, forever shines anew,
Each moment shared reaffirms our vow,
In your love, my heart finds solace now.

I won't give up though hardships abound,
For in loving you my resilience is found,
In your eyes my soul revives its fire,
With you, my love, I'll never tire.

Through life's turmoil, our love stands tall,
A testament to our unyielding call,
To rise, to face, to conquer and to be
Together, victorious, wild and free.

In your love, my heart beats anew,
Faith incarnates forever true,
With every breath, I'll love you till the end,
Together, our bond will forever transcend.

Twilight

As twilight descends, soft and serene,
My heart beats fast for the unseen,
In hues of pink and gold, it sets aflame,
A beauty that my soul cannot explain.

Like unspoken love, it whispers low,
A gentle breeze that only few may know,
A longing gaze, a heartfelt sigh,
A feeling that cannot be denied.

The sky is painted like a masterpiece so fine,
A blend of day and night divine,
The stars appear like diamonds that shine bright,
A celestial show beyond all might.

In twilight's hush, I find my peace,
A sense of calm, my worries are released,
Like secret love, it wraps me tight,
A warm embrace on this enchanted night.

The world is bathed in a golden glow,
A soft caress that only love can show,
The trees stand tall, like sentinels of old,
Guarding the moments, forever to be told.

Oh, twilight's beauty, you speak to me,
In whispers of a love yet set to be free,
A language known only to the heart,
A symphony that is heard never to depart.

In twilight's silence, I hear your call,
A whispered promise that echoes through it all,
A love so pure, so true and kind,
A feeling that is forever mine.

So let me bask in twilight's gentle light,
And cherish the love that shines so bright,
For in its beauty I'll find my way,
To the secrets of the heart that beat each day.

Dusk and Dawn

As dusk descends with shadows dark and deep,
My heart feels lost in love's troubled sleep.
The stars hide beneath a sombre and sullen veil,
Reflecting the turmoil, the struggles I hail.

The world outside a fading dying light,
Echoes the sorrow through the dark night.
The path ahead, uncertain and unclear,
Leaves me searching and yearning, dispelling all
the fear.

But then the dawn with a promise slowly breaks,
A new beginning unfolds; an old castle of
despair shakes
The sun rises high with a radiant and golden
glow,

Illuminating a hope filled with love's reviving
flow.

So let us cherish the dusk's quiet night,
And welcome dawn's awakening with all its
light.
For in this cycle of life's highs and lows,
Lies the promise of love that will forever glow.

From dusk till dawn, our hearts beat strong,
Enduring the struggles, righting the wrong.
With every breath, a new chance unfolds,
To love, to live, to rise above life's turmoil, bold.

In this dance of dusk and dawn, we find our
way,
Through life's dark moments, to a brighter day.
So hold on to hope, through the darkest night,
For with the dawn, new light, new love, takes
flight.

Vision of you

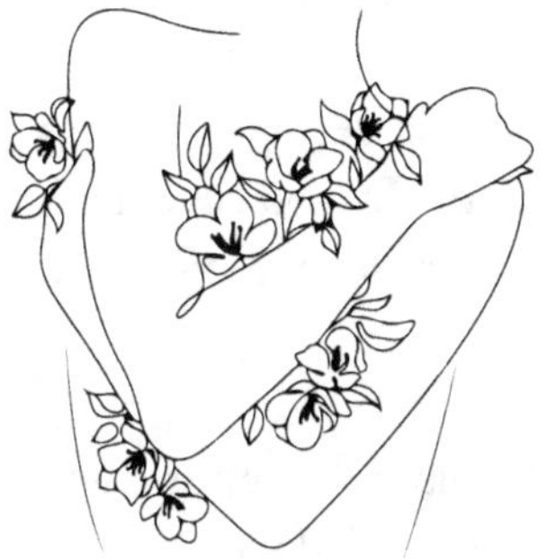

In twilight's hush where shadows play,
When stars begin to shine a vision to sway,
Delicate and exotic I see a beauty so rare,
A symbol of my love beyond compare.

Like petals of a flower, soft as a lover's sigh,
Your glance unfurls the eternal sky,
A palette of hues in shimmering dance,
You move with grace in a romantic trance.

Like love's first blush your colors unfold,
A gentle warmth that I so long to hold,
Your delicate curves, a work of art divine,
A reflection of nature's intricate design.

In your elegance I find you as my own,
The beauty expressed in every tender tone,
I find your presence in unexpected places,
A feeling so familiar that fills the spaces.

As my desire for you stems unfettered and
strong,
I write our story in destiny's sweet song.
That will last forever and echo through time,
A testament to our love that you are forever
mine!

Like the roots that dig deep and wide,
The depths of our bond won't subside,
Through life's turmoil your love remains steady
in my heart,
A beacon of hope that never departs.

So I call onto you as a flower of might,
A symbol of my strength in the darkest of night,
Your beauty reminds me of a hope that never
died,
Standing in the rain a flame that burns so bright.

Saranghae: A Love So True

In the land of morning calm and serene night,
Where words are spoken from the heart's
delight,
There's a phrase that defines love so fine,
'Saranghae', a term that's truly divine.

It's more than just a mere word or two,
It's a promise, a vow, a love that shines through,
A declaration of devotion so pure and true,
Uncovering a heart's deepest feeling to
something new.

When spoken softly with gentle care,
It heals the soul leaving no room for despair,
For in its essence an emotion so strong resides,
A bond that ties two hearts, side by side.

Walking in the stillness of the night,
Under the stars that twinkle with delight,
A lover's whisper heard with a heartfelt sigh,
It represents a love that is endless like the sky.

With every breath, with every heartbeat,
This love phrase speaks directly to the heart's
repeat,
A rhythm of passion, a symphony of fire,
That burns within, a love that never tires.

In the chaos of life's busy streets,
Where words are lost and love retreats,
'Saranghae' stands tall like a beacon bright,
Guiding lovers through life's darkest night.

So let us cherish this phrase so dear,
A symbol of love, that casts away the fear,
For in its beauty one sees the life pass by,
In the sweet melody of 'Saranghae', you never
ask why!

www.ingramcontent.com/pod-product-compliance
Lightning Source LLC
La Vergne TN
LVHW050912200726
843508LV00011B/2186